Stop Biting Your Tongue

Ashly Colosimo

BookLeaf Publishing

India | USA | UK

Presentation by *BookLeaf Publishing*

Web: www.bookleafpub.com

E-mail: info@bookleafpub.com

ISBN: 9789363304611

First edition 2024

PREFACE

Trigger Warning!
These poems speak about mental health, suicide, and addiction. This book is unfiltered and contains strong language.

Drowning in a Drought

How do I begin?
How do I tell you every thought and emotion
that's flowing through my head,
like the water in this tub, I'm nearly drowning in.
How do I look you in the eyes, and tell you I'm
fine,
as the blood seeps out from this thin razor line

How the fuck did I get here?
These demons that hide in my mind,
right when I think it's alright they come for yet
another fight.
Anxiety, depression, social conformity
drugs addiction stress, and death,
what the fuck am I supposed to do next!

Block out the pain you are feeling.
Smile! That's what you should be doing.
You should be moving on,
you should get your degree,
you should live your life,
why can't you just be happy?
These are the things they say to me,
along with the "he said she said,"

the rumors about me and him that constantly
spread,
like "I heard...."
Stop!
Don't tell me, I don't want to hear it.
Don't tell me what you think I should do,
what I could have; should have done if only I
were you.
Don't tell me you understand and hold out a
helping hand,
then pull it away like some sick twisted plan.
As if I haven't tried like hell to rise above this,
you remind me that you're just another snake,
and I didn't hear the hiss.
Don't tell me you'll be there for me, no matter
what whatever I need
you and I both know someday you'll leave me,
petrified of the demons that hide inside,
intertwined with my nightmares, stuck on
rewind,
but don't worry,
I'm fine.

You see the words you said helped ease the
blade,
into the skin, I'd sworn to never mark again.
I sit with burning white clenched hands,
I'll relax and reach for the damn pen instead.
I'll write my thoughts on the page,

telling you how I've come so far, but yet still
self-degraded.
My eyes will cry until this darkness fades,
until my body stops shaking with rage
until the guilt I carry is finally paid.
I'll write until I free my mind from this cage.

You see Daddy always told me we have
addictive tendencies,
that alcohol and I should remain sworn enemies,
but somewhere down the line, I picked up a
dependency,
until I drank myself sick.
Thinking Holly shit is this really me?
Pale skin, black eyes, makeup streaking down
my face,
wondering if I gave up would I be a disgrace,
to my family to my friends to myself.
Wondering if I'm even worthy of God's help.

You see my mind is the enemy, it's a very scary
space.
My heart isn't in it I don't want to continue this
chase,
someone help I just need a break,
and I'm left wondering why the fuck,
I chose to dance with this devil in the first place.

Memories of the Mute

Mamma says talk about it,
as she opens the door to my personal hell.
Mamma says talk about it,
it might make you feel better.
We can get you help if you want it.

Mamma,
how do I tell you the nightmare of my reality
stuck on replay?
How do you tell you about that day
without opening the closet I've tried to
barricade?

Let's talk about it.
It was another long day,
I was exhausted.
It was long past my bedtime.

I sent a half-glance smile to the one who held
my heart
begging without words for him to come to bed
with me.
Right on cue he smiled and said,
"Be right there."

I laid down.
Feeling the instant relief of being off my aching
feet
Admiring the peace and quiet.
It was deafeningly quiet.
Like a fire alarm at 3 am,
my heart dropped to my stomach.
Something was wrong, I couldn't deny it.

I got up and ran searching for him.
Searching for some kind of noise,
because this house is so fucking
silent.
Screaming into the darkness
with only silence echoing back at me,
mocking my fears into my reality.

As if I should have known,
as if I should have been faster,
as if it were my fault.
Happily never ever after.

His blue lips,
pale face,
grey body,
lay before me.

Heart racing,
hands shaking,

thoughts spacing,
think!
Think!
Think!
The only heartbeat I can make out is my own.

Medics are asking questions,
lots of questions,
I'm speechless.
Shaking.
Scared.
Looking like a deer in headlights,
Paralyzed.
Stunned,
like a bad accident you can't seem to look away
from.
It's like slow motion,
watching the bullet leave the gun.
Yet, I don't move.
I wait for it to hit me,
hoping it will shock my body back into reality.

It's okay.
Breathe.
That's all they keep saying.
The silence of the waiting room is haunting.
Alone my thoughts get the best of me.
What if...
I could have...

I should have....
But the silence continues to echo.

Waiting for some kind of news,
after fourteen hours, the chairs' paisley print and
my tears
have smeared into the water painting.
A distraction from the headache
that came when my eyes opened their
floodgates.

Thoughts hijacking my mind
I have no fight left.
Did I tell you I love you before bed?
Did I tell you I loved you...

You know it's bad when an atheist hits their
knees,
and bows their head.
Praying.
Bargaining for some kind of second chance.
Thinking.
Why me?
Why him?
Why now?
Where are you now God!?
Where are you now?

The days go by with the daily hospital routine.

Cry.
Pray.
Sleep.
Repeat.
Cry.
Pray.
Sleep.
Repeat.
Beep. Beep. Beep. Doctors.
Beep. Beep. Beep. Doctors.
Day in, day out.
Twenty-six days like clockwork.

The beeping continues,
the doctors come in with hollow faces
that have been perfected by protocol.
Followed by bad news, hugs, and sorry.

"No.
Wait.
No.
I'm in denial.
No this can't be happening.
Wake up! Wake up!
Why won't you wake up!"

Hands holding.
Hearts breaking.
Voice shaking.

It's okay.
Beep beep beep goes the monitor.
I love you.
Beep beep beep.
Goodbye love.
Beeeeeeep

Mamma says talk about it,
but Mamma doesn't know it was an overdose.
After twenty-six days of noise and chaos,
the world stopped turning.
As we bowed our heads
for a moment of silence.

Frozen in Time

Thirty:
Compressions.
One, and two, and three
five, and six, wait four,
count!
nine and ten.
Eleven?

Two:
Rescue breaths were placed upon your blue lips.
Watching your chest rise and fall,
then back to compressions.

Ten:
Minutes of CPR and finally your lungs take a
breath.
But your mind wasn't on the same page.

Fifteen:
Minutes you were unconscious before I found
you.
Maybe twenty,
maybe ten.
I don't know.

Five:

Minutes after losing consciousness causes fatal
brain damage.

I was too late.

Twenty-six:
Days spent at the hospital holding your hand,
I talked to you every day,
But I never got the answers I needed.
I begged, I bargained, I pleaded.
Twenty-six days I listened to the monitor's beep,
watching a different doctor rush in.

Three:
A.M. I held your hand,
I told you how much I loved you,
as I said a final goodbye, to my dear friend.

Four:
Weeks I didn't get out of bed.

One:
Year later,
time keeps moving,
but I'm stuck in one place.

Ten:
Years later,
I'm starting to be okay.

Awaiting Daylight

The pen moves along the page, but these words
don't hold meaning.
My thoughts are going wild, voices in my head,
all screaming.
As I sit on this bed at a quarter to two,
this room is so dark, but the moon is still
beaming.

This feeling, like a rush, like a tickle, so
unexplainable.
I gave you my heart, begging you to be careful.
It's delicate, fragile, breakable.
I gave you parts of me that are irreplaceable.
If only these memories were erasable.
They haunt me at night, they're unshakable.

I've laid here for days staring at the ceiling
Hoping the world will forget while I lie here
dreaming.
My body has gone numb, I'm left with no
feeling.
I guess this is what happens to a broken heart.
They call this "healing."

Above all, it's about having no regrets.

It's hard not to regret when you can't seem to
forget.
Please let me die here, I don't want to face the
world yet.
Not till I can walk along, and not cry every time
I pass where we first met.

Keep Going

They tell me I should run,
or maybe try to write.
They don't see the struggle,
the constant battle,
the endless fight.

They paint this picture in my head that things
will be okay,
but what no one understands is the pain from
just one day
I try to be strong.
I do it all, I even pray,
but when it's all said and done,
the pain never really goes away.

They don't understand that some days are harder
than others.
The challenge to wake up becomes more of a
struggle.
You don't know what it's like to have your world
fall apart.
To hold someone's hand as the machine stops
pumping their heart.
To see the doctors constantly checking their
charts.

Knowing there's nothing more anyone can do,
that's the hardest part.

There is no greater pain than putting a lover in
the ground.
But what's worse, is the silence that follows,
not a sound.
Don't get me wrong,
I live the best I can,
it's just hard to face reality.
We had a love, we had a plan.

Thank You For Trying

You Did The Best You Could
I know you did the best you could, given what
you had.
That doesn't change the outcome of events.
Neither good nor bad.

You did everything you could.
How could I have known?
You were here to help,
I thought I had to find myself on my own.

You found a flashlight!
With dead batteries.
You found solar panels!
On a rainy day.
Will I ever find my way?

You found sparklers!
Without matches,
candles with no wicks,
just melted waxes,
You caught lightning bugs
that refused to shine.
It's almost like this was by design.
You looked for stars

on cloudy nights.
You longed to bring me something bright.

I couldn't see that you were trying.
All the effort you had been applying.
Just to guide me back home,
when the sun had stopped shining.

You did the best you could, given what you had.
That doesn't change the outcome of events
Neither good nor bad.

Too Afraid To Fall

It's like,
When you're standing on the edge,
below you is joy and adventure,
behind you is expectations and standards.
Every time I find myself at the edge,
I never jump.
I turn around.
The path I'm on must be a circle,
because sooner or later the edge will be closer.

Everyone is telling me to jump,
as I stand on the edge,
the girl who once climbed to the top of a tree,
just to see the view,
has suddenly developed a fear of heights.

Maybe that's why they say you fall in love.
Maybe something pushes you over the edge.
As I stand on this ledge,
I'll debate once again,
on turning around or falling in.

Ruminations Between Dusk to Dawn

These days drag on like they will last forever,
so we take our time awaiting our last endeavor.
The sun will come up for a brand new day,
but for some, it's the endless night that will stay.

We won't say goodbye because we fear it will
last,
but the deed has been done and that is that.
We won't shed a tear, there is no time to waste,
our lives are flying by and some can't keep up
the chase.

So take hold of your dreams and own them this
time.
No one can take them away unless you step out
of line.
The emotions that flood you will drown you in
thoughts,
but the one on my mind is the only one that I've
got.

I think of my life as if it is over
because I can't stand the feeling of being sober.
So I drink down another and lose myself again,

the sun won't always come up my friend.

Take a seat as your life flies by,
you lost all that you had,
because you were ready to die.

Stay With Me

I've been staring at this page for hours,
with a mess of thoughts filling my head.
I've replayed every memory,
every last word you ever said.

I know this game,
where you say sweet things
to get in my bed.
So is this another game?
Am I being misled?

I hate these days when I sit here asking why.
It feels like I'm waiting for you to leave without
a goodbye.
Though you're still here, I have no reason to cry.
I don't understand why these tears are pooling in
my eyes.

Pull me in and hold me tight,
please don't let go, not tonight.
Let's cancel our plans,
we'll stay in until everything is alright.
We can light some candles, dim the lights
Say you love me, more than you did before.
Take my hand,

show me the world we still have to explore.
Kiss me, say you need me more.

Don't just say you love me
Make me believe you
Stop and remember how much we have been
through.
I don't know about you, but my feelings are true.
There will always be a place in my heart for just
you.

Suicide Is Silent

Take me back to where it all began.
Let's figure this out, we will come up with a plan
I don't have much to offer, but I'll give you all I
can.

I won't sleep, not tonight.
Not till I know you'll be alright.
Not till I've entered the darkness and shined
some light.
I won't let you go, not without a fight.

Stay here, with me, for just one more day.
I'll find a way to make you want to stay.
I'm not religious but I'll hit my knees and pray
Maybe that will help, in the slightest way.
Please darling please, I beg you don't give up
Don't walk away.

Even in the silence, your words ring through my
ears,
they cut the soul, deep, they bring me to tears.
You have broken the walls, that had once stood
for many years.
You unlocked the gate, unleashing my fears.

I can't sit here and let you face this world alone,
I would have come sooner if I had only known.
Why didn't you call me?
Why didn't you answer your phone?
I was too late.
Now I stand here over your tombstone.
I'll blame myself for not seeing the signs you
hadn't shown.

Stop Biting Your Tounge

He catcalled her!
"Hey! Hey, Sexy!"
She chuckled at the joke
not wanting to become the punch line.
"I'd like to see what you're working with.
Mhhmmm girl you're perfect."

She could have said "thank you," and walked
away.
Stay poised like a lady is supposed to be.
But she was getting sick of catcalls,
from
#SaturdaysAreForTheBoys,
egocentric dicks.
Instead, she decided to shut him down real
quick.

She looked him right in the eyes, gave him a
smirk, and thought..
My body is not going to shimmy and shake into
too-tight skinny jeans,
that squeeze my thighs so tight it looks like I'm
walking with a goddamn stick up my ass.
My body likes
#Sweatpants.

My body will not wear push-up bras
To make my almost (A) cups into barely (B)
cups.
I will not flat iron my hair just to style it how
you like.
My hair is nappy, unbrushed, I've got shit to get
done.
#MessyBun
My body does not take kindly to starvation.
My body has scars, my body has bruises,
my body has stories that don't seem to interest
you.
My body will not be touched for your pleasure,
my body is my God-given temple.

Imagine his reaction,
a combination of rage and embarrassment.
She would catcall him back
"Hey, superficial asshole!
You want my attention?
Compliment my achievements, determination,
my spirit, my mind, my confidence, and strength
my attitude, my charm, my dedication!
Admire ME next time!
Not my body!

But instead,
She said "Thank you,"
then walked away.

Ode To Band-Aid Boys

I ran into you,
accidentally,
but thinking back it was intentional.
So I could get your attention.

You caught my half-glance smile from across the
room,
and assumed I was looking at you.
You took your chance,
hit me with a,
"Hey, I couldn't help but message you,
I think you're cute."

Have you played this game before?
You should have known better,
we only hang out behind closed doors.
I got off by messing with your head,
convinced you this was love,
when I was only your friend in bed.

You pressed your too-heavy body on top of me,
begging me to strip between your sheets,
asserting yourself between my knees.
Each night would soon turn to day.
We would never speak of our secret game,

I'm sorry you're just another pawn to play.

You knew I was toxic,
It was never going to be a fairytale with you and
me.
I suppose maybe you just longed for company,
someone to keep your heart wanting,
even if in the end, it meant nothing.

SHE

She fucked you up, didn't she?
She played with your heart,
Maybe hurt your feelings.
She broke you down,
mentally, and emotionally.
She,
the one you loved before me.

I bet you were really in love.
When your hands intertwined, they'd fit like a
glove.
I bet she was the only thing that mattered.
That was until your heart was shattered.

She played games with your feelings, didn't she?
Told you she'd always be there,
then turn around to leave.
She conjured up these dreams with you,
as you lay together in bed.
Now they're nightmares on replay stuck in your
head.

I bet she knew what you liked.
Kisses down your neck held you real tight.
I bet she promised you forever.

You never thought she'd leave that same night.

She told you she loved you, didn't she?
You gave her your heart, unconditionally.
For her, you would have done anything,
she fucked you up, didn't she?

You.
You fucked me up.
Mentally and emotionally.
You told me to come over,
then told me to leave.
You told me you loved me,
but only between your sheets.

I was never enough for you.
You took your pain and you put it on me.
She fucked you up,
And you fucked up me.

I Think Of You

I wonder if I ever cross your mind,
the way you seem to still cross mine.
I wonder if when you fight with her you miss
me,
I wonder if I slip into your dreams on those
lonely evenings.
I wonder if you ever search my name
privately check on me from miles away.

I wonder if you ever thought about reaching out.
Probably not, we'd have nothing to talk about.
I wonder if she makes you happy.
I wonder if leaving you will always be the
biggest mistake I made.

I wonder if you ever remember those days,
I wonder if they ever stick in your mind on
replay.
I wonder what you'd think of me now.

I will always remember you as the one who tried
to save me from myself
I will never be able to thank you for that.
You will always remember me as the girl,
who broke you for no good reason.

I didn't mean to, my sharp edges cut you too.
I wasn't ready for you then, I'm sorry for that.
My long lost best friend.

Passion Vs. Perception

You say "I don't know how to communicate"
Yet, ask my opinion like it holds the most
weight.
You come to me when you want someone to tell
you straight.
It's a game of cat and mouse,
you lay the trap, I take the bait.

You like to say I'm unprofessional.
Like my vocabulary and tone are unacceptable,
but my directness is commendable.
My words are carefully chosen, each is
intentional.

You keep saying I'm too loud,
I'm making too much noise and disrupting the
crowd.
If the crowd follows my lead why aren't you
proud?
Or is it because you'd rather I take a bow?
Allow you to be the face, keep my voice down.

I've never understood why people sugarcoat
their words

Always have to question if the conversation is
off the record
Why beat around the bush?
I bet you'd say what's on your mind if I really
start to push.

You said, "I'm proud of you for working on your
communication skills."
What you meant was,
thank you for getting quiet, your words give me
chills.
What you mean is,
deep breath in, deep breath out, and practice the
drills.
What you meant was,
to take down the passion we don't want the thrill.
Your mind is too quick please be still.

There is no need to yell, everyone is listening.
Do you hear the clock tick? Time is dwindling.
I can't read between the lines,
say it or start distancing
Shhhhh!
They call this anxiety,
when my heart rate and word speed start
quickening.

If you're going to say it, say it with your chest.

What a world we would live in if every
conversation wasn't a test.
Always miscommunicating thoughts versus
feelings,
this is a mess.
Stop.
Write it down.
Give it a rest.
You say I can't communicate.
What you mean is,
you're not ready to hear what I have to say.

To My Lover

You asked why I never write poems about you.
I'm not a love poet dear,
I write about the trauma I've been through.
That's not fair,
a memory gets more attention than you do
So listen up, these feelings, they're all true.

I told you I wasn't a love poet
I don't want to love you through a page,
I want to show it.
I had a lot of healing to do,
I know you know it,
For you, I try my best.
From girlfriend to fiance, to wife,
For you, I commit.
I've been so afraid of losing you, it's hard to
admit.

I never wrote about you, I never had words for
this feeling.
All my troubles all my sorrows you've been
stealing,
picking up all the slack and grief I've been
dealing

I've been walking the steps, they call this
healing.

How do I put into words what you mean to me?
I had locked up my heart you had gone and
found the key.
I had pushed you away, but you still got down
on a knee.
I wish I could see the woman you seem to see.

I don't write poems about us because we live in
the present.
I write through the past, hindsight is
twenty-twenty,
I write poems to vent.
I try to decipher every conversation and what it
might have meant.
But you love, I've never had to do that.
You darling are heaven-sent.

Working Class Culture

There is a welcome mat at the entrance
but you're not welcome here.
There is a smile that greets you at the door
but that smile hides her fear,
from men who long to touch her,
men who call her dear.
She'll never drop her armor
she'll never drop a tear,
but yet these men are welcome here,
and so she lives in fear.

There are cracks in the foundation
The walls are caving in.
Tenants seek other homes for salvation
no one will let them in.

There are fist-sized holes punch through the
walls,
everyone whispers through the halls,
and we all walk on eggshells,
waiting for this house of cards to fall.
There is no time to rest,
you live on 24/7 call.

Screams still echo behind closed doors,

and another battle rages on.
Attempts to settle the score,
check your words at the door,
don't slip, and don't start another war.
Hold your tongue,
your honesty is uncalled for.

The picture frames hang crooked,
fitting for those within.
Someone get us out of here
send help, do not come in.

There are no beds to lay our heads,
the stress keeps us wide awake.
For all that we are willing to give, they continue
to take.
Another day, another task, another thing to make
us break.
By now we should have let this house fall,
but there's too much at stake.

There are cracks in the foundation,
the house is caving in.
Someone call a fireman,
this house should be condemned

I cannot stay here any longer,
There is coke out on the table.
Was this a joke, I surely hope

wouldn't want to get a label.
Someone help!
Our tenants are unstable.

Birthday Commencement

Congratulations to the newborn class!
Welcome to the land of the living!
You didn't choose this day,
you didn't choose this era.
But it's your turn to forge your own way.

This journey won't be easy.
You will stumble along the way
But here is some advice
A guide to help you, through those darker days.

Congratulations newborn class,
lesson one begins.
You must learn to find your voice.
This world is full of noise.
You must demand to be heard,
you have no other choice.

On to lesson two.
You may be learning to walk, talk,
or even tie your shoes.
This stage may be frustrating,
everything is new.
Keep your mind open,
learning is all you have to do.

Prepare to make some friends,
not all will be kind to you.
This stage may be hard,
you may struggle to fit in.
We were not all born identical,
we are not all barcodes on a box.
You were never meant to fit in,
it's okay to feel a little lost.

When you get to the teen years,
it's all about pretend.
No one has a clue what to do,
don't be fooled,
no one has a plan.
You aren't meant to figure things out
before you've had the chance to begin.
Give yourself the grace
to find the colors of the wind.

Many will try to tell you the best way to be,
the way to live, the job to get, and what you
should believe.
Take this as a chance to listen,
but do not blindly follow.
This journey is yours, my dear
keep dreaming of your own tomorrow.

Now when you think you've made it,
appreciate the struggle.

Each new chapter will bring
new challenges to juggle.

This body you are trapped in,
it's only just a shell.
Don't be angry with its change,
speak kindly to your body,
it's been with you through every stage.

Sometimes, you may be at war,
with the mind body, and spirit.
There doesn't need to be a winner,
each piece just wants you to feel it.
Feel the emotions, and listen to the thoughts,
then process them and talk them out,
each will teach you a lot.

Congratulations to the newborn class,
your time starts now.
This life is a paradox both long and short
somehow.
It's your turn,
make only yourself proud!

Table for Two

When I was young,
Life and I were best friends.
We'd talk about the future,
With vast dreams and prudent plans.
As Life and I grew on together,
Life began to taunt me.
Life became ruthless.

Life and I have since been in a complicated
relationship.
Life has let me down a great deal in the past,
but I always seem to give Life infinite chance.

Life wanted to make it up to me,
insisting I come over for dinner.
Life was cooking up an overflowing pot of
anguish on the stove,
with adversity in the oven.
Life went heavy on the spices.
rue, affliction, malice, and despair.

Life said, "Have a seat, bow your head for
prayer."
Life served me a heaping plate of grief with a
side of fortitude.

Life says "You are what you eat."
It was time for me to leave,
but I didn't want to be rude.
Life sensed fears left unspoken,
reminding me that Death's door is always open.
Life is funny like that,
mocking my affection towards Death.

I got up to leave; reminding Life it was to blame.
Life insisted I stay, maybe we could play a
game.
I shot Life a livid glare,
because Life loves games,
but does not play fair.
Life served me a helping of grief with a side of
fortitude.
I left Life sitting at a table set for two,
as I knocked on Death's door,
for a final meal I couldn't refuse.

Undiagnosed

I am Undiagnosed
Spiraling in and out between my perception and
reality.
I imagine this is what it feels like to be a ghost.
Caught between two worlds,
so far away from home,
but still feel so close.

I am Undiagnosed
My symptoms unexplained
Is it masking?
Is it mania?
Is it stress?
Or just pain?
The stakes are high with everything to lose,
mental clarity to gain.

My mental health is a battle,
Making relationships strained.
Lately, my thoughts have been roaming,
No longer able to be contained.
What a shame they'll say. What a shame.

Maybe I'm autistic,
symptoms include the inability to read the room.

Saying things bluntly,
as a matter of fact,
but always perceived as being rude.
I can't read your social ques
the lights are too bright,
the music to loud,
I got overstimulated,
I snapped at you.
I'm sorry, you don't understand,
I didn't mean to....

Maybe I'm bipolar,
symptoms include fluctuating mood swings,
manic episodes of high highs,
doing crazy things.
Feels like I'm a puppet,
not in control of my own strings.
Impulsive, irrational, risky,
can you imagine the consequences this behavior
brings?

Maybe I have anxiety,
excessively worrying about things I cannot see.
Listing all the reasons, pros, and cons, it'll never
be.
Constant fight or flight, always running,
always trying to flee.
Someday I hope my symptoms are explained.
Maybe a diagnosis will set me free.

I wonder If it's ADHD.
Is that why I talk so fast?
Answer questions that nobody asked.
Fidget in my seat, watching the clock,
waiting for time to pass.

I wonder if a diagnosis will help me understand.
Why my mind play games that I can't stand.
My thoughts race, I can't comprehend,
why I have a hard time making friends.
I wonder if a diagnosis would give me the
answers I'm looking for.
Maybe someday my mind and body will end
their war.
Will these symptoms ever silence,
can they ever be ignored?

I am an undiagnosed neurodivergent.
At times it feels like every thought,
every feeling, everything is urgent.
I'm learning to be present,
trying to stay in the current.
Always monitoring my moods,
trying to stay observant.
I can't explain what it feels like to be
neurodivergent,
maybe someday I'll be sane.
I hope someday I get to explore it.

Anxiety

Before I understood anxiety,
I couldn't put into words the war raging inside
me.
How truth was only valid based on what I could
see,
like broken bones, bruises, and scrapped knees.

How does one explain what's affecting you
physically and mentally?
You've tried calling out for help but no one hears
your plea.
How do I explain the Intrusive thoughts in my
mind?
Like I want to do great things and see the
sunshine,
but in the same thought contemplate suicide.
Sometimes I feel my inner thoughts are Dr.
Jeckle and Mr. Hyde.
A story if you will, not sure which version is
mine.

How does one explain anxiety to their partner,
when's the right time?
Every conversation plays out in my head like,
Speak, pause, rethink, rewind.

Anxiety is the alarm that alerts the body.
The heart starts racing like you drank too much
coffee
Thoughts begin spacing, speech is spotty.
The problem with anxiety is the alarm is faulty.
There's no need to panic, there's no real
emergency.
But at this moment, and in my mind, this is fight
or flight
You vs. Me.

I'm learning how to live with anxiety.
Taking frequent walks and writing poetry.
Learning to reset the mind and body,
with cold showers, and speaking intentionally.
Anxiety alarms are loud inside, but often present
quietly.
Here's to learning the difference between what is
me,
and what is my anxiety.

www.ingramcontent.com/pod-product-compliance
Lightning Source LLC
LaVergne TN
LVHW021254200726
843509LV00012B/1666